CULTURE
— IN THE —
CLASSROOM

Standards, Indicators, and Evidences for Evaluating Culturally Responsive Teaching

A PUBLICATION OF SERRC - ALASKA'S EDUCATIONAL RESOURCE CENTER

Southeast Regional Resource Center (SERRC) Project CREATE was funded by an Alaska Native Education Program Grant, CFDA 84.356; OESE, U.S. Dept. of Education, Award #S356A120021-13.

www.serrc.org

www.culturallyproficientschools.org

PROJECT CREATE STAFF

Gerry Briscoe - Director
Martha Gould-Lehe - Cultural Specialist
Dan Henry - Educational Specialist
Marianne Shealy Dobbs - Educational Specialist

SERRC Juneau Office
210 Ferry Way
Juneau, AK 99801
(907) 586-6806

SERRC Anchorage Office
805 W. 3rd Avenue
Anchorage, AK 99501
(907) 349-0651

For additional resources visit:

www.culturallyproficientschools.org

CONTENTS

OVERVIEW

Research has established the importance of cultural proficiency in improving students' academic and behavioral outcomes. Effective educators recognize that culture influences their actions as well as the thoughts and behaviors of their students (Nuri-Robins, Lindsey, Lindsey & Terrell, 2012). To ignore the impact of one's culture is to ignore the opportunities and challenges within the instructional teaching and learning environment. Culturally responsive teaching practices can assist educators in bridging differences in language, heritage, race, socio-economic status, trauma history, and ability. As a result, educators are realizing the need to intentionally focus on identifying effective methods for developing culturally responsive practices.

Cultural proficiency is a mindset. When considered this way, it becomes an active, evolving journey that school leaders and educators undertake to cross philosophical barriers toward thoughtful and reflective school change. Systematic change has the best chance of creating and sustaining learning environments where students achieve and realize their full educational potential, and educators can self-reflect to ensure their beliefs and attitudes are free of bias.

Culture in the Classroom: Standards, Indicators and Evidences for Evaluating Culturally Proficient Teaching was created for the purpose of self-reflections and continuous improvement by teachers, and for evaluation and feedback by evaluators.

This document was developed as part of SERRC's Project CREATE to develop and support a teacher evaluation framework aligned with research-based instructional models such as Marzano's Art & Science of Teaching, and Danielson's Framework for Teaching. Project CREATE has elaborated on the Alaska Cultural Standards for Educators to develop indicators and evidences upon which teachers can be evaluated for culturally- responsive instruction.

Culture in the Classroom complements other state standards by orienting the school community to its role in helping students become responsible, capable, and whole human beings. Culture in the Classroom emphasizes a strong connection between what students experience in school, and their lives out of school, by providing in-depth, experiential learning in real-world contexts.

School Districts and personnel will find this publication useful in assisting educators in the teacher evaluation process. It provides examples of what culturally responsive instruction and practice could look like. Teachers will also find it helpful in planning for meaningful, effective lessons, activities, and strategies that meet the cultural standards for educators.

This document applies to all evaluation and instructional frameworks, and is inclusive of all cultures. Evidences and indicators are broad enough to allow for each teaching site to localize activities, lessons, and practices to fit their specific and unique needs.

ACKNOWLEDGEMENTS

On behalf of Southeast Regional Resource Center (SERRC), and Project CREATE we take great pleasure in thanking the consultants who worked with Project CREATE staff to create the cultural descriptions, indicators, and evidences.

CONSULTANTS:

Sperry Ash – Educator: Cultural Specialist: Nanwalek
Kris Busk - Coordinator of Instructional Support: Bering Strait School District
Barbara Cadiente-Nelson- K-12 Native Student Success Coordinator and Grant Administrator for Title VII: Juneau School District
Carol Gho – Retired Math Professor; Cultural Consultant: Fairbanks
Daniel Greenwood – Educator: Anchorage School District
Sonta Hamilton-Roach - Educator: Iditarod School District
Nedra (Jana) Harcharek – Director Inupiaq Education Department: North Slope Borough School District
Esther A. Ilutsik- Director of Yup'ik Studies: Southwest Region School District
Janice Littlebear – Retired Educator; Lead Mentor-Curriculum Developer Alaska Statewide Mentor Project University of Alaska Statewide
Megan Mickelson – Cultural Integration Specialist: Kodiak Island Borough School District
Stacey Paniptchuk – Educator: Bering Strait School District
Susan Paskvan – Native Language Coordinator: Yukon-Koyukuk School District
Nita Reardon - Retired Educator; Cultural Consultant: Homer
Nita Towarak - Retired Educator; Cultural Consultant: Unalakleet

---

SERRC would also like to thank the Advisory Board Members for their diligent and hard work in providing advice, guidance, resources, and support to develop, implement, and sustain the project's work.

PROJECT CREATE ADVISORY BOARD MEMBERS:

Sheryl Weinberg – Executive Director, Southeast Regional Resource Center
Clarence Bolden, Retired North Star Borough School District Human Relations Director
Walkie Charles, PhD, Assistant Professor of Alaska Native Language Program and Linguistics, University of Alaska Fairbanks
Sonta Hamilton-Roach, Educator, Iditarod School District
Mary Huntington, Principal, Bering Strait School District
Aaron Iworrigan, School Board Member, Bering Strait School District
Alberta Jones, Assistant Professor of Education, University of Alaska Southeast
Chris Simon, Rural Education Coordinator, Alaska Department of Education and Early Development
Nita Towarak, Retired Educator, Unalakleet
Carl White, Special Assistant to the Superintendent, Bering Strait School District

Cultural Standards and Indicators for Teacher Evaluation

Cultural Standard A	Cultural Standard B	Cultural Standard D	Cultural Standard E
Culturally responsive educators incorporate local ways of knowing and teaching in their work.	Culturally responsive educators use the local environment and community resources on a regular basis to link what they are teaching to the everyday lives of the students.	Culturally responsive educators work closely with parents to achieve a high level of complementary educational expectations between home and school.	Culturally responsive educators recognize the full educational potential of each student and provide the challenges necessary for them to achieve that potential.
CA1 The educator plans lessons that incorporate knowledge of students' cultural background/practices into the teaching of content.	**CB1** The educator has a planning process that incorporates the linking of the local environment, community resources, and issues to instructional content.	**CD1** The educator plans culturally sensitive ways to build relationships with parents/guardians to achieve complementary expectations of students.	**CE1** The educator plans for academic rigor that will challenge each student regardless of cultural background.
CA2 The educator integrates and connects traditions, customs, values, and practices of the students when interacting with new content.	**CB2** The educator engages students in learning experiences that integrate the local environment, community resources, and issues when interacting with content.	**CD2** The educator communicates with homes to better understand the student's educational needs, concerns, and strengths.	**CE2** The educator provides rigorous learning opportunities for students that combines higher order thinking skills and student autonomy (from teacher-directed to student-directed).
CA3 The educator's uses the students' cultural traditions, customs, values and practices when designing the classroom environment.	**CB3** The educator reflects on the effectiveness of using the local environment, community resources, and issues to help students connect content to their daily lives.		**CE3** The educator demonstrates value and respect for all students of all cultures and challenges them to strive for educational excellence.
CA4 The educator uses students' traditions, customs, values, and practices to engage them in their learning.	**CB4** The educator seeks guidance regarding the local environment, community resources, and issues and how it connects to the everyday lives of the students		**CE4** The educator reflects on student performance based assessments, both formative and summative to identify areas for academic rigor.
CA5 The educator reflects on the effectiveness of applying their knowledge of students' traditions, customs, values, and practices when teaching.			
CA6 The educator seeks guidance regarding knowledge about and use of students' traditions, customs, values, and practices when teaching.			

Standard A: Culturally-responsive educators incorporate local ways of knowing and teaching in their work.

Standard B: Culturally-responsive educators use the local environment and community resources on a regular basis to link what they are teaching to the everyday lives of the students.

Standard C: Culturally-responsive educators participate in community events and activities in appropriate and supportive ways.

Standard D: Culturally-responsive educators work closely with parents to achieve a high level of complementary educational expectations between home and school.

Standard E: Culturally-responsive educators recognize the full educational potential of each student and provide the challenges necessary for them to achieve that potential.

Cultural Standard A
Cultural Connections

A. Culturally-responsive educators incorporate local ways of knowing and teaching in their work.

Description of the Standard:

Cultural Standard A addresses incorporating knowledge of students' culture into an educator's pedagogical practice. Educators should strive to know about the cultural background and heritage of the students they teach. The educator uses this knowledge in their teaching practice to engage and anchor students in their learning. Knowledge of students' background and heritage should guide the choices educators make about strategies and practices they use with their students.

Focus Statement	Desired Outcome
The educator uses students' cultural traditions, customs, values, and practices in their teaching.	Educators are guided by their knowledge of students' background and heritage when making decisions about strategies and practices they will use in their teaching.

Indicator #	Cultural Indicator	Reflection Question
CA1	The educator plans lessons that incorporate knowledge of students' cultural background/practices into the teaching of content.	How will I include more cultural traditions, customs, values and practices of the students in my classroom when I plan?
★CA2	The educator integrates and connects traditions, customs, values, and practices of the students when interacting with new content.	How will I incorporate the local traditions, customs, values and practices when teaching new content?
★CA3	The educator's uses the students' cultural traditions, customs, values and practices when designing the classroom environment.	What can I do to make my classroom environment more representative of the culture(s) of my students?
★CA4	The educator uses students' traditions, customs, values, and practices to engage them in their learning.	What more can I do to use the cultural traditions, customs, values, and practices of my students to effectively engage them?
CA5	The educator reflects on the effectiveness of applying their knowledge of students' traditions, customs, values, and practices when teaching.	What evidence do I have that incorporating the students' culture into my lessons is effective?
CA6	The educator seeks guidance regarding knowledge about and use of students' traditions, customs, values, and practices when teaching.	How and from whom will I seek advice for the appropriate use of students' traditions, customs, values, and practices in my teaching?

★*Denotes indicators that can be observed in the classroom.*

Indicator #	
CA1	The educator plans lessons that incorporate knowledge of students' cultural background/practices into the teaching of content.

Desired Outcome
Educators' plans include references and/or activities and assignments that connect to students' backgrounds and heritage for the purpose of improving student achievement and increasing student engagement.

Example Evidences of Planning

- ❑ Educator's unit plans include specific activities and assignments that connect students' backgrounds and heritage to the content.
- ❑ Educator can show evidence of data collection, related to students' backgrounds and heritage. (i.e. parent surveys, student bios, etc.)
- ❑ Educator analyzes data collected about students' backgrounds and heritage and uses it for planning.
- ❑ Educator planning includes scheduling of community members to support connecting students' backgrounds and heritage to the content.
- ❑ Educator can explain the process used to gather information about students' cultural heritage and backgrounds.
- ❑ Educators incorporate information gathered about students' cultural backgrounds into written lesson plans.

Rating Scale			
Unsatisfactory	*Basic*	*Proficient*	*Exemplary*
The educator's plans do not incorporate knowledge of students' cultural background(s)/practices into the teaching of their content.	The educator incorporates knowledge of students' background into the planning process, however there isn't a statement of how the activity, lesson, or reference will connect to the content.	The educator incorporates knowledge of students' background into the planning process, and there is a statement of how the activity, lesson, or reference will connect to the content.	The educator's plans use the students' cultural background(s) in unique and creative ways to make connections to the content.

Indicator #	
⭐CA2	The educator integrates and connects traditions, customs, values, and practices of the students when interacting with new content.

Desired Outcome
Students make connections between their cultural backgrounds and new content.

Example Student Behaviors	Example Educator Behaviors
❑ Students discuss their traditions, customs, values, and practices and how it relates to new content. ❑ Students are highly engaged. ❑ Student artifacts demonstrate cultural connections to the content being taught. ❑ Students can explain how the content connects to their cultural background and heritage.	❑ Educator uses previewing activities and or relevant "hooks" to help students make connections between content and their traditions, customs, values, and practices. ❑ Educator involves community guests to illuminate connections between content and the students' traditions, customs, values, and practices. ❑ Educator can describe how cultural connections within the unit contribute toward understanding of the content. ❑ Educator integrates cross-curricular cultural connections to content. ❑ Educator asks questions of students that require students to make inferences between their cultural background and content.

Rating Scale			
Unsatisfactory	Basic	Proficient	Exemplary
The educator's use of cultural traditions, customs, values, and practices was not appropriately connected to the introduction of new content.	The educator makes cultural connection(s) to the content but the majority of the students cannot state how the connection relates to their cultural traditions, customs, values, and practices.	The educator makes cultural connection(s) to the content and the majority of the students can state how the connection relates to their cultural traditions, customs, values, and practices.	The educator makes cultural connections to the content in unique and creative ways so that all students were able to state how the content connects to their cultural backgrounds.

Indicator #	
★CA3	The educator uses the students' cultural traditions, customs, values and practices when designing the classroom environment.

Desired Outcome
Students can recognize representation of their culture in the physical environment of the classroom

Example Student Behavior	Example Educator Behaviors
❑ Students can describe how their traditions, customs, values, and/or practices are represented in the classroom, i.e. work products, posters, routines, etc. ❑ Students can explain how the classroom environment makes them feel comfortable, safe, included, valued, and respected.	❑ Educator involves members of community to participate in classroom design. ❑ Educator displays interpretations and/or cultural products of student work that reflect the students' traditions, customs, values, and practices. (student work) ❑ Educator incorporates the traditions, customs, values, and practices of students represented in the classroom in their visual displays and decor. (i.e. posters) ❑ Educator includes the traditions, customs, values, and practices of students into the development of classroom routines and rules. ❑ Educator provides cultural resources on a regular basis, i.e., books, web sites, brochures, speakers, that students can access.

Rating Scale			
Unsatisfactory	*Basic*	*Proficient*	*Exemplary*
The educator's use of students' cultural traditions, customs, values and practices in the design of the classroom environment was not used appropriately.	The educator uses cultural knowledge of students' cultural traditions, customs, values and practices in the design of the classroom, but the majority of students cannot recognize representation of their culture in the physical environment of the classroom.	The educator uses cultural knowledge of students' cultural traditions, customs, values and practices in the design of the classroom, and the majority of students can recognize representation of their culture in the physical environment of the classroom	The educator uses knowledge of students' cultural traditions, customs, values and practices in unique and creative ways in the design of the classroom, and all students recognize representation of their culture in the physical environment of the classroom.

Indicator #		
★CA4	The educator uses students' traditions, customs, values, and practices to engage them in their learning.	

Desired Outcome

Students are highly engaged and motivated to learn as a result of connections to their traditions, customs, values, and practices.

Example Student Behavior	Example Educator Behaviors
❑ Students participate in activities that incorporate their traditions, customs, values, and practices with learning content. ❑ Students can tell how making cultural connections to content is engaging. ❑ Students' non-verbal body language expresses engagement.	❑ Educator uses activities related to traditions, customs, values, and practices of the students in their class, i.e. music, language, foods, etc. ❑ Educator demonstrates awareness of the nonverbal communication appropriate to the customs of the students in their classroom. ❑ Educator has discussions with students about topics in which they are interested. ❑ Educator builds student interests into lessons.

Rating Scale

Unsatisfactory	Basic	Proficient	Exemplary
The educator does not use students' traditions, customs, values, and practices to engage students with the content.	The educator uses the students' traditions, customs, values, and practices, but the majority of students do not display engagement and/or motivation to learn.	The educator makes connections between the students' traditions, customs, values, and practices, and the majority of the students are engaged and motivated to learn.	The educator uses cultural connections to students' traditions, customs, values, and practices in unique and creative ways so that all students are engaged and motivated to learn.

Indicator #	
CA5	The educator reflects on the effectiveness of applying their knowledge of students' traditions, customs, values, and practices when teaching.

Desired Outcome
Through reflection, educators can identify ways to become more culturally responsive in their teaching.

Example Evidences

- ❑ Educator identifies this indicator as an area for personal growth.
- ❑ Educator documents the steps they have taken toward personal growth in this indicator. i.e.. logs, journals, actions plans, etc.
- ❑ Educator identifies observable measures that would demonstrate growth in this indicator. i.e. benchmarks, timelines, student data.
- ❑ Educator identifies a goal(s) for this indicator.

Rating Scale			
Unsatisfactory	*Basic*	*Proficient*	*Exemplary*
The educator lacks reflection on his/her teaching and therefore does not identify ways to become more culturally responsive in their teaching.	The educator reflects on how to use students' traditions, customs, values, and practices but does not identify specific ways to become more culturally responsive.	The educator reflects on how to use students' traditions, customs, values, and practices and identifies specific ways to become more culturally responsive.	The educator reflects on how to use students' traditions, customs, values, and practices and how to adapt culturally responsive practices in order to reach all students in the classroom.

Indicator #	
CA6	The educator seeks guidance regarding knowledge about and use of students' traditions, customs, values, and practices when teaching.

Desired Outcome
The cultural content is accurate and credible, and the delivery correctly follows cultural protocols.

Example Evidences

- ❏ The educator understands that they need to seek out protocols for guidance in cultural knowledge.
- ❏ The educator adheres to the cultural and intellectual property rights that pertain to all aspects of the local knowledge by citing and documenting resources.
- ❏ The educator keeps a record of specific instances when and from whom they sought mentorship.
- ❏ Educator consults with community members to guide and support planning that incorporates students' cultural backgrounds and heritage with the content.
- ❏ Educator collaborates with staff when planning to incorporate students' cultural backgrounds in their teaching.

Rating Scale			
Unsatisfactory	*Basic*	*Proficient*	*Exemplary*
The educator does not seek guidance in the use of or the knowledge of students' cultural traditions, customs, values, and practices.	The educator seeks guidance in the use of cultural information relating to students' traditions, customs, values, and practices but the information used is not accurate or the delivery of the lesson does not follow cultural protocols.	The educator seeks guidance in the use of cultural information relating to students' traditions, customs, values, and practices and the information used is accurate and the delivery of the lesson does follow cultural protocols.	The educator seeks guidance and collaborates with peers and community members to ensure accurate information of cultural content in their teaching.

Cultural Standard B
Authentic Local Resources

B. Culturally responsive educators use the local environment and community resources on a regular basis to link what they are teaching to the everyday lives of the students.

Description of the Standard:

Cultural Standard B addresses the educator using the authentic environment on regular basis as a bridge to new learning. The authentic environment is the local community that all students are members of regardless of their cultural heritage. The resources available for an educator may include people, environment, businesses, and organizations (hospitals, clinics, corporations, etc.). Educators that successfully link the authentic environment with the curriculum help students develop connections between content and their everyday lives.

Focus Statement	Desired Outcome
The educator regularly uses local resources helping students make connections between the content and their everyday lives.	Students connect classroom learning to their daily lives.

Indicator #	Cultural Indicator	Reflection Question
CB1	The educator has a planning process that incorporates the linking of the local environment, community resources, and issues to instructional content.	How can I improve my planning process to be more inclusive of the local environment, community resources, and issues with instructional content?
★CB2	The educator engages students in learning experiences that integrate the local environment, community resources, and issues when interacting with content.	What can I do to broaden my understanding of the local environment and community resources so that I can help my students interact with knowledge/content more effectively?
CB3	The educator reflects on the effectiveness of using the local environment, community resources, and issues to help students connect content to their daily lives.	What evidence do I have that incorporating the local environment, community resources, and issues are helping my students connect content with their everyday lives?
CB4	The educator seeks guidance regarding the local environment, community resources, and issues and how it connects to the everyday lives of the students.	How and from whom will I seek guidance about the appropriate use of local resources?

★*Denotes indicators that can be observed in the classroom.*

Indicator #		
CB1	The educator has a planning process that incorporates the linking of the local environment, community resources, and issues to instructional content.	

Desired Outcome
Educator's plans include references and activities connecting content to the local environment.

Example Evidences

- ❏ Educator's plans reflect using the local environmental resources on a regular basis; i.e. speakers, field
- ❏ Educator's plans integrate the content standards with cultural standards utilizing local resources.
- ❏ Educator's plans reflect the use of the local environment's seasonal activities; i.e. traditional uses of resources for different seasons.
- ❏ Educator's plans includes elements to make connections between the students and the local environment, i.e. field trips, guest speakers, out of doors, activities, etc.

Rating Scale			
Unsatisfactory	*Basic*	*Proficient*	*Exemplary*
The educator's plans do not incorporate knowledge of the students' local environment, community resources, and issues in the teaching of their content.	The educator incorporates knowledge of students' local environment, community resources, and issues into the planning process, however there isn't a statement of how the activity, lesson, or reference will connect to the content.	The educator incorporates knowledge of students' local environment, community resources, and issues into the planning process, and there is a statement of how the activity, lesson, or reference will connect to the content.	The educator's plans use the students' local environment, community resources, and issues in unique and creative ways to make connections to the content.

Indicator #		
⭐ **CB2**		The educator engages students in learning experiences that integrate the local environment, community resources, and issues when interacting with content.

Desired Outcome

Students make connection between their local environment, community resources, community issues and the content.	

Example Student Behaviors	Example Educator Behaviors
❑ Student artifacts reflect the knowledge of the local environment. ❑ Students demonstrate interest and engagement when using the local environment and or resources. ❑ Students' attitudes and or behaviors demonstrate respect for the local community resources; i.e. respecting land area, personal property, other persons, etc.	❑ Educators' activities/ assignments facilitate making connections to the local environment and culture. ❑ Educator uses the local environment, i.e. out-of-doors lessons, field trips, place based investigations, etc. ❑ Educator organizes students to interact with the local resources being presented; i.e. groups, prepared questions, graphic organizers, etc.

Rating Scale

Unsatisfactory	Basic	Proficient	Exemplary
The educator's use of the local environment, community resources, and/or issues was not appropriately connected to the introduction of content.	The educator makes cultural connection(s) to the content but the majority of the students cannot state how the connection relates to the local environment, community resources, and/or issues.	The educator makes cultural connection(s) to the content and the majority of the students can state how the connection relates to the local environment, community resources, and/or issues.	The educator makes cultural connections to the content in unique and creative ways so that all students are able to state how the content connects to the local environment, community resources, and/or issues.

Indicator #	
CB3	The educator reflects on the effectiveness of using the local environment, community resources, and issues to help students connect content to their daily lives.

Desired Outcome

Educator monitors effectiveness of using authentic local resources as a result of student learning.

Example Evidences

- ❑ Educator can explain the effectiveness of strategies used to make cultural connections.
- ❑ Educator maintains records on how the local environment, community resources, and issues are being incorporated into lessons.
- ❑ Educator uses informal student assessments to evaluate the effectiveness of incorporating the local cultural environment and/or resources.
- ❑ Educator debriefs with peers, presenter, students, etc. to gain feedback on successes, challenges, or changes.

Rating Scale

Unsatisfactory	Basic	Proficient	Exemplary
The educator lacks reflection on his/her teaching and therefore does not identify ways to become more effective in using the local environment, community resources, and/or issues to connect content to students' daily lives.	The educator reflects on how to use the local environment, community resources, and/or issues but does not identify specific ways connect content to students' daily lives.	The educator reflects on how to use the local environment, community resources, and/or issues and identifies specific ways to connect content to students' daily lives.	The educator reflects on how to use the local environment, community resources, and/or issues and how to adapt them to connect content to students' daily lives.in order to reach all students in the classroom.

Indicator #	
CB4	The educator seeks guidance regarding the local environment, community resources, and issues and how it connects to the everyday lives of the students.

Desired Outcome

Educator accurately uses authentic community resources and cites sources used.

Example Evidences

- ❑ Educator maintains records of their efforts to seek guidance on using authentic local resources.
- ❑ Teacher participates in continuing education courses and/or workshops that help them learn about local resources and issues.
- ❑ Educator has a mentor that shows or tells them what is the correct use of local areas and/or resources.
- ❑ Educator meets with the guest presenters in advance of their visits to preview content and/or to clarify expectations.

Rating Scale

Unsatisfactory	Basic	Proficient	Exemplary
The educator does not seek guidance in the use of or the knowledge of the local environment, community resources, and/or issues.	The educator seeks guidance in the use of cultural information relating to the local environment, community resources, and/or issues but the information used is not accurate.	The educator seeks guidance in the use of cultural information relating to the local environment, community resources, and/or issues and the information used is accurate.	The educator seeks guidance and collaborates with peers and community members to ensure accurate information of the local environment, community resources, and/or issues in their teaching.

Standard C is not mandated for evaluation since it cannot be observed in the classroom. Nevertheless, many school districts have adapted Standard C to make it a part of their teacher evaluation.

Cultural Standard C
Community Connections

C. Culturally-responsive educators participate in community events and activities in appropriate and supportive ways.

Description of the Standard:

Cultural Standard C addresses the importance of educators being connected to their students' environments, and developing relationships with the people who interact with them in those environments. Although this standard isn't part of an educator's evaluation because it isn't observable in the classroom, it is the cornerstone standard. All four of the other cultural standards depend upon the educator building a knowledge base about their students and developing meaningful relationships within the community so the educator is perceived as a contributing member who respectfully gleans knowledge about the students' "place".

Indicator #	Cultural Indicator
CC1	Become active members of the community in which they teach and make positive and culturally appropriate contributions to the well being of that community.
CC2	Exercise professional responsibilities in the context of local cultural traditions and expectations.
CC3	Maintain a close working relationship with and make appropriate use of the cultural and professional expertise of their co-workers from the local community.

Cultural Standard D
Home Connections

D. Culturally responsive educators work closely with parents to achieve a high level of complementary educational expectations between home and school.

Description of the Standard:

Cultural Standard D addresses the collaboration between home and school so there is mutual support for the expectations of the student. The word complementary in the standard is defined as, combining in such a way as to enhance the qualities of each other. Based on this definition, both the educator and the parent share a responsibility in communication and support of the student's educational expectations. The educator seeks parent/guardian input and acts upon their concerns so that the student's educational needs are met and supported. Educators should maintain open communication with parents regarding educational expectations for students and feedback on student progress. It is the educator's responsibility to persistently work with all parents, including those who are less involved with the educational process, to provide suggestions/resources to parents, which help promote student success.

Focus Statement	Desired Outcome
The educator works collaboratively with parents in coordinating efforts to support student expectations.	Parents and the educators cooperate to support the child's education.

Indicator #	Cultural Indicator	Reflection Question
CD1	The educator plans culturally sensitive ways to build relationships with parents/guardians to achieve complementary expectations of students.	What will I do to strengthen my relationship with parents/guardians to ensure that expectations set for students are mutually supported and understood?
CD2	The educator communicates with homes to better understand the student's educational needs, concerns, and strengths.	How will I collaborate with parents/guardians to learn about student strengths and discover areas of need or concern?

Indicator #	
CD1	The educator plans culturally sensitive ways to build relationships with parents/guardians to achieve complementary expectations of students.

Desired Outcome

Educator learns and uses culturally sensitive ways to develop relationships with all parents.

Example Evidences

- ❑ Educator communicates with parents in ways that are culturally responsive. (i.e. translators, web based translation of newsletters)
- ❑ During teacher/parent interactions, parents are informed of upcoming plans, and are invited to participate.
- ❑ Parents visit the classroom.
- ❑ Classroom physical environment reflects an attitude that parents are welcome.
- ❑ Parents contribute as classroom helpers, etc.
- ❑ The educator demonstrates integrity, confidentiality, respect, flexibility, fairness, and trust when building relationships with parents.
- ❑ Educator responds to parent requests for support, assistance and/or clarification regarding their child in a timely manner.
- ❑ The educator uses technology to build collaborative relationships between home and school.
- ❑ Educator can produce evidence of furthering their understanding of the culture, ie. reading material, classes, professional learning groups, etc.

Rating Scale

Unsatisfactory	Basic	Proficient	Exemplary
The educator's plans do not reflect culturally sensitive ways to build relationships with parents/guardians.	The educator plans culturally sensitive ways to interact with parents/guardians, but does not work toward building complementary expectations with the parent for the student.	The educator plans culturally sensitive ways to interact with the majority of parents/guardians, and builds complementary expectations with the parent for the student.	The educator plans ways to interact with *all* parents/guardians and adapts culturally sensitive strategies that support and respect families in achieving educational outcomes for students.

Indicator #	
CD2	The educator communicates with homes to better understand the student's educational needs, concerns, and strengths.

Desired Outcome

The educator uses information about students' backgrounds to meet student needs.

Example Evidences

- ❏ Educator's plans show multiple ways to get input from families. (family night, emails, web site, conferencing, phone calls, surveys, etc.).

- ❏ Educator seeks to continuously learn about and build upon the cultural knowledge that students bring with them from their homes and community.

- ❏ Educator plans for the needs of students who come from home environments that offer little support for schooling.

- ❏ When assigning homework, the educator takes into consideration the students' family resources.

- ❏ Educator can describe instances when he or she interacted positively with students and parents.

- ❏ Students and parents can describe positive interactions they have had with that educator.

- ❏ When communicating with the home, the educator takes into consideration family and language resources.

- ❏ Educator maintains an web-based site where assignments, upcoming events, etc are posted for student-home access.

- ❏ Educator is culturally sensitive and consistent in communicating with the home regarding expectations, progress, and/or concerns.

Rating Scale

Unsatisfactory	Basic	Proficient	Exemplary
The educator communicates with homes but does not gather information about the home environment.	The educator communicates with homes and gathers information about the home environment, and uses that knowledge to meet some students' educational needs.	The educator communicates with homes and gathers information about the home environment, and uses that knowledge to meet the majority of the students' educational needs.	The educator communicates with *all* home environments, and uses that information to meet the educational needs of *all* students.

Cultural Standard E
High-Unbiased Expectations

E. Culturally responsive educators recognize the full educational potential of each student and provide the challenges necessary for them to achieve that potential.

Description of the Standard:

Cultural Standard E addresses the belief by the educator that all children can learn. Educators support high expectations for all students by recognizing the cultural integrity and identity students bring with them into the classroom, and by reflecting on their own practices and beliefs. The educator engages students with respect, cultural sensitivity, and confidence in each student's ability to learn. Educators maintain high expectations for all students by: resisting making judgments based on stereotypes; using strategies that support all learners; and monitoring all students for achievement of the learning goals.

Focus Statement	Desired Outcome
The educator recognizes all students of all cultures can achieve and will provide rigorous academic challenges for them.	All students believe they can achieve and will strive to meet the challenges of academic rigor.

Indicator #	Cultural Indicator	Reflection Question
CE1	The educator plans for academic rigor that will challenge each student regardless of cultural background.	What will I do to better understand the full potential of each of my students in order to challenge their learning?
★CE2	The educator provides rigorous learning opportunities for students that combines higher order thinking skills and student autonomy (from teacher-directed to student-directed).	How can I guide and support all students of all cultures to demonstrate higher order thinking skills and develop student autonomy?
★CE3	The educator demonstrates value and respect for all students of all cultures and challenges them to strive for educational excellence.	How can I cultivate a classroom environment that encourages all students to strive for academic excellence and show pride in their culture?
CE4	The educator reflects on student performance based assessments, both formative and summative to identify areas for academic rigor.	How do I differentiate my instruction to support diverse student learning needs?

★ *Denotes indicators that can be observed in the classroom*

Indicator #	
CE1	The educator plans for academic rigor that will challenge each student regardless of cultural background.

Desired Outcome

The educator delivers instruction that is scaffolded and differentiated to challenge and meet the needs of all students.

Example Evidences

- ❑ Educator's plans have differentiation strategies that reflect cultural sensitivity. (i.e. wait time, grouping, environment, learning styles)
- ❑ Educator's plans regularly include cultural connections to students in the classroom.
- ❑ Educator's plans include assessment strategies to measure student progress that accommodate cultural diversities.
- ❑ Educator's plans build on student background knowledge to address cognitive complexity.
- ❑ Educator designs strategies/activities that explicitly use the verbs associated with complexity. ie., Bloom's Taxonomy.

Rating Scale

Unsatisfactory	Basic	Proficient	Exemplary
The educator's plans do not reflect strategies and activities that are rigorous and/or culturally sensitive to challenge and meet the needs of all students.	The educator 's plans reflect strategies and activities that are culturally sensitive but lack rigor in order to challenge and meet the needs of students.	The educator 's plans reflect strategies and activities that are rigorous and culturally sensitive to challenge and meet the needs of the majority of students.	The educator 's plans reflect strategies and activities that are rigorous and culturally sensitive to challenge and meet the needs of *all* students.

Indicator #	
★ CE2	The educator provides rigorous learning opportunities for students that combines higher order thinking skills and student autonomy (from teacher-directed to student-directed).

Desired Outcome

Students exhibit higher order thinking and increased student autonomy.

Example Student Behaviors	Example Educator Behaviors
❑ Students participate in large and small groups and in various roles within those groups. ❑ Students are engaged in higher order activities (i.e.problem based learning or project based learning) ❑ Students engage in critical thinking discussions that connect various cultural perspectives to the topic.	❑ Educator organizes students in various ways to interact with content. ❑ Educator uses strategies that challenge students to apply their knowledge in creative ways, ie. problem solving, examining similarities and differences, etc. ❑ Educator facilitates culturally responsive discussions allowing students to apply critical thinking skills.

Rating Scale

Unsatisfactory	Basic	Proficient	Exemplary
The educator does not structure learning opportunities for students to demonstrate higher order thinking skills and/or student autonomy.	The educator structures learning opportunities for some students to demonstrate higher order thinking skills and develop student autonomy.	The educator structures learning opportunities for the majority students in order for them to demonstrate higher order thinking skills and develop student autonomy.	The educator structures unique and creative learning opportunities for *all* students in order for them to demonstrate higher order thinking skills and develop student autonomy.

Indicator #		
CE3	The educator demonstrates value and respect for all students of all cultures and challenges them to strive for educational excellence.	

Desired Outcome

All students feel capable, worthy, and accepted by the educator.

Example Student Behaviors	Example Educator Behaviors
❑ Students take risks. (i.e. ask questions, participate in discussion, volunteer) ❑ Students state the teacher cares about them. ❑ Students exhibit a willingness to learn. ❑ Students avoid negative thinking about their abilities, attitudes, and actions. ❑ Students are willing to accept challenges. ❑ Students persevere with higher order learning activities. ❑ Students demonstrate respect toward others and property. ❑ Students display positive attitudes and actions in the classroom.	❑ Educator treats all students fairly. ❑ Educator interacts with students in culturally responsive ways, ie. smiles, makes appropriate physical contact, understands nonverbal signs, etc. ❑ Educator promotes inclusion of diverse cultures. ❑ Educator models respect for all students. ❑ Educator encourages students to achieve their full potential through scaffolding and/or differentiation. ❑ Educator addresses students in a manner they perceive as culturally respectful, i.e. using their Native name (if appropriate), not talking too loudly, not demanding eye contact, playful dialogue, etc. ❑ Educator maintains an environment that is safe. ❑ Educator does not allow negative comments about student' abilities and provides strategies for students to use to avoid negative thoughts and actions.

Rating Scale

Unsatisfactory	Basic	Proficient	Exemplary
The educator encourages some of the students to persist in difficult and challenging learning experiences and interacts with them fairly and equitably.	The educator encourages the majority of the students of *all* cultures to persist in difficult and challenging learning experiences and interacts with them fairly and equitably.	The educator encourages *all* students of *all* cultures to persist in difficult and challenging learning experiences and interacts with them fairly and equitably.	The educator uses unique and creative ways to encourage *all* students of *all* cultures to develop leadership skills while collaborating with peers to solve real world problems.

Indicator #	
CE4	The educator reflects on student performance based assessments, both formative and summative to identify areas for academic rigor.

Desired Outcome
Educator analyzes formative and summative assessments and differentiates instruction to challenge and meet the needs of all students.

Example Evidences

- ❑ Educator reflection journals.
- ❑ Educator pulls from multiple sources of data to create an Individual Learning Plan that includes the student's culture.
- ❑ Student growth goals.
- ❑ Educator tracks student progress toward specific goals.
- ❑ Educator engages in purposeful conversations about the students to identify areas of need and possible solutions/interventions. (i.e. former teachers, parents, paraprofessionals, cooks, janitors, other school staff as appropriate, RTI process.)

Rating Scale			
Unsatisfactory	*Basic*	*Proficient*	*Exemplary*
The educator reflects on students' assessments but lacks follow through to develop strategies that consider the student's culture when identifying strategies for increasing academic rigor and identifying areas of need.	The educator reflects on student's assessments to determine the effectiveness of instruction, but does not develop strategies that consider the student's culture when identifying strategies for increasing academic rigor and identifying areas of need.	The educator reflects on students' assessments and determines the effectiveness of specific strategies and considers the student's culture when identifying strategies for increasing academic rigor and identifying areas of need.	The educator is creative and innovating in developing an Individual Learning Plan for each student based upon assessments and the student's culture.

CPSIA information can be obtained
at www.ICGtesting.com
Printed in the USA
LVHW071009210120
644269LV00012B/398